July 4, 1982

To Michael –

from

Grandpa and

Grandma Aiken

The Color Nature Library
ZOO ANIMALS

By
FRANK W. LANE

Designed by
DAVID GIBBON

Produced by
TED SMART

CRESCENT BOOKS

To John, Jean and Anne—
may they enjoy their work
as much as their father
enjoys his.

First published in Great Britain 1977 by Colour Library International Ltd.
Designed by David Gibbon. Produced by Ted Smart.
© Text: Frank W. Lane. © Illustrations: Frank W. Lane.
Colour separations by La Cromolito, Milan, Italy.
Display and Text filmsetting by Focus Photoset, London, England.
Printed in Spain by Grijelmo, S. A.
Published by Crescent Books, a division of Crown Publishers Inc.
All rights reserved.
Library of Congress Catalogue Card No. 77-17745
CRESCENT 1978

INTRODUCTION

"After the wilds of Africa how can you bear to photograph in zoos?" It's a fair question, to which there are several answers.

A greater variety of animals can be photographed in one day in a large zoo than in a year (or years!) in the wild. Moreover there are some animals, such as the denizens of the tree-tops in dense jungles, and creatures which lurk in waters far from the under-water photographers' domain, which are virtually impossible to photograph except in captivity.

You can also get nearer to your subject in a zoo than is generally possible in the wild. And purely from a photographic point of view there is little, if anything, to distinguish a close-up of an animal in captivity from one in the wild. The secret is to obtain a result which looks as natural as possible.

Zoos are certainly popular. In Great Britain annual attendances approach 20 million; throughout the world nearly 350 million. By far the world's most popular zoo is in Mexico City: seven million visitors each year. Entrance is free. The zoo with the largest collection of animals is in West Berlin. In 1976 it had 12,531 animals (including 4,788 invertebrates) of 2,315 species.

Despite the criticisms levelled at zoos, no-one seriously interested in animals would wish to see them abolished. Apart from their value in breeding new stock, the educational value of zoos is immense. If there were no zoos there would be an incalculable loss of interest in the animal kingdom. Would that matter? Here is the answer of Sir Peter Chalmers Mitchell, the distinguished Secretary of the Zoological Society of London from 1903 to 1935.

"Every civilised nation spends great sums on painting and sculpture, on libraries and museums. Living animals are of older lineage, more perfect craftmanship and greater beauty than any of the creations of man.

Nowhere else than among living animals are there such strange fantasies of colour, such play of light on contour and surface, such intimate relation between structure and form. They provide a rich material for the anatomist, histologist, physiologist, parasitologist and pathologist. They are an endless laboratory for the student of psychology; they are the basis of the study of zoology; their study is a necessary adjunct to the study of man in health and disease."

I would add this to what Sir Peter so eloquently expressed: it will be a poorer world if the time ever comes when children have to ask: "What was a lion?"

There is a real danger of that pathetic question being asked. Look what happened to the tiger, one of the most magnificent animals ever to walk this earth. It is estimated that in 1920 there were some 100,000. In 1976 there were scarcely 2,000.

Is it generally realised that since the 17th century nearly 100 species of birds and over 50 species of mammals are known to have become extinct? The actual number of species which have perished in that time is almost certainly greater. It is a fair assumption that some species have been lost before there was time for them to be added to the zoological lists. The classic of all bygones, the dodo, was kept in zoos but there is no record of any attempt to breed them.

There are ever-increasing pressures on animals in their natural state. The reclamation of swamplands, the cutting down of forests, the encroachment of domestic animals on wild animal reserves, however understandable in the short term, mean fewer wild animals. It is a sadly ironic fact that the countries with the most rapidly increasing human populations, and consequently increased demand for agricultural land, are also the countries where wildlife is most abundant.

Zoologists to whom I have spoken believe the time is fast approaching when it is the zoos of the world which will have to maintain the world's wild animal population. Whether or not this position is ever reached, it is a fact that already there is a two-way traffic in wild animals: not only from the wild to zoos but also <u>from</u> zoos to the wild. In 1947 only 50 Hawaiian geese were left in the world. Four were collected and carefully protected. In 1950 two of their offspring were supplied to the Wildfowl Trust at Slimbridge. But they both laid eggs, so in 1951 a gander was supplied. When he died in 1963 he was the ancestor of nearly 250 Hawaiian geese! Today the Trust supplies Hawaiian geese to zoos throughout the world–and has sent some to Hawaii.

Another species that has been saved by captive breeding is the European bison or wisent. The last wild specimen died in 1925 but, fortunately, at that time there were some 50 wisents in captivity and from these the species has been saved; there are about 600 today. Père David's deer is extinct in the wild but specimens exist in many zoos. And there are many more Przewalski's horses in captivity than in their native Mongolia.

Zoo directors would like to abolish the old-fashioned cage for large animals. Many zoos now confine them by moats. All animals should be provided with as nearly natural conditions as is reasonably possible, an important requirement for successful breeding.

At Borasparken in Sweden the African section contains a mixed collection of rhinoceroses, zebras, giraffes, gnus, cranes, hornbills, ostriches and guineafowl, all roaming freely. In the Vogelpark at Walsrode in Germany the sea-birds' enclosure not only has a beach and a "sea," but also mechanically induced waves which constantly beat against the shore.

The largest aviary in the San Diego zoo is, in effect, a miniature rain forest, containing many full-grown trees in which hundreds of birds live an almost natural life. And in the Frankfurt zoo the penguin enclosure reproduces the frigid conditions of Antarctica. I know–I have photographed in this ice-house.

The ideal way to keep large animals is to allow them to roam in open-range zoos in rural surroundings. The prototype of such zoos is Whipsnade–Sir Peter Chalmers Mitchell's brainchild–embracing 567 acres–on the top of the Bedfordshire chalk downs.

No pretence is made that this book breaks new ground in either zoology or photography. But I hope it will have some zoological value in stimulating interest in the many excellent zoos which exist today, and photographic value in showing what can be accomplished by relatively simple 35mm. equipment–by someone who did not take up professional photography until he was past sixty.

A King Penguin *left*.

The Wild Cat, *left* found in the forests of Africa, Europe and West Asia, may look like the domestic cat but it is virtually untameable. Twenty-six mice were once found in the stomach of one Wild Cat.

There are a number of different geographical races of tiger. They are distinguished by colour, size and markings. The Sumatran Tiger *previous page* is one of the smallest and is now restricted, in the wild, to two areas of Sumatra.

The Amur Leopard *right* lives farther north than any other of the species, reaching into the Amur region of Russia. The hair is long and thick and the coat is marked with large spots.

The Northern Lynx *below* of the northern forests of Europe, Asia and North America, is a solitary beast which hunts by night. Prey is mainly hares, rabbits, birds and small deer, but other fare is welcome, including squirrels, fish and beetles. The only animal a lynx has to fear is man – lynx fur is valuable.

8

Young Cheetahs of Africa have different colouring from the adults. The young *left* also have a silver mane which runs the whole length of the back, but this disappears before they are three months old.

The African Lion *right*, once common throughout the Old World – including Europe – is now confined to Africa south of the Sahara. Lions appear to take readily to captivity (one lived in the Cologne Zoo for twenty-nine years) and breed well.

The very rare Asiatic Lion *below* is now confined to the Gir Forest in north-west India. In 1908 it was estimated that there were only thirteen in existence; today there are about three hundred.

One of the most beautiful of all living mammals is the Indian Tiger *left*. The average weight is about five hundred pounds but one shot near the Chinese border weighed eight hundred and fifty-seven pounds–a record weight for any member of the cat family. A hungry tiger can, in one meal, eat food equal to a fifth of its body weight.

The Serval, of Africa, *right* lives in thick grass and bush near water. Here it stalks a variety of prey from rodents to lizards, hares to young antelopes. Servals are extremely agile and have been known to snatch low-flying birds out of the air.

Living in the highlands of the central Asian mountains the Snow Leopard *below* sometimes ascends to eighteen thousand feet. As an adaptation to its cold habitat the Snow Leopard's fur is exceptionally long, some two inches thick on the back and four on the belly. They prey on goats, sheep, deer and other mammals, hunting generally at twilight or during the night.

Found in many parts of Africa and Asia, the Leopard *right* is the most widely distributed of all the big cats. It is very agile; climbing trees, jumping, running or swimming as occasion demands.

The Leopard Cat *top left* is about the same size as the domestic cat although with much longer legs. It is an Asian species and is common in India.

Panthers are fairly common in Southeast Asia. The Black Panther *above* is a melanistic, or dark, form of the leopard.

The Caracal *left* of Africa and Asia is a solitary, mainly nocturnal animal which preys on small antelopes, hares and birds.

Rat Snakes *left* are widely distributed in both the Old and New Worlds. They are often found in trees. In addition to rats, they eat other small mammals and birds, killing their prey by constricting.

Non-venomous, the European Grass Snake *right* is semi-aquatic and eats frogs as well as mice and birds.

The apparently sluggish appearance of the Green Tree Boa *below* of South America is deceptive. So swift is the strike that birds are occasionally caught.

A Polar Bear sometimes grows to an enormous size; one specimen killed in Alaska weighed almost a ton. They are dangerous animals and have been known to stalk, kill and eat humans.

An inhabitant of the temperate forests of the Northern Hemisphere, the Brown Bear *overleaf, left* varies greatly in size and colour. Specimens from Alaska sometimes measure ten feet and weigh three-quarters of a ton. Prey is killed, not by hugging, but by powerful blows with the fore-limbs – armed with dagger-like claws.

The strikingly marked Himalayan Black Bear *overleaf, right* ranges up to twelve thousand feet. It hibernates in caves or hollow trees.

Geckos vary greatly in size, from about one inch to over a foot long. The beautifully marked Madagascan Gecko *top left* is fond of lurking in coconut palms, waiting for insect prey, but it also eats bananas and oranges. The undersides of Geckos' feet have pads furnished with tiny bristles–some with microscopic suckers–which enable them to cling to all but the most polished surfaces. Geckos often invade human dwellings and eat insects which are attracted by house lights.

Living in the trees of the American tropical forests, the Common Iguana *right* takes readily to water when alarmed. Its diet is entirely vegetarian. Although it measures up to six feet in length it is far from being the largest of the lizards. The Komodo Dragon of Indonesia grows to a length of ten feet and a weight of about three hundred and fifty pounds. Even this reptilian giant is dwarfed by the extinct dinosaurs. The longest measured about ninety feet; the heaviest one hundred tons!

Water Lizards *centre left* of South America live alongside jungle streams. These lizards are good swimmers and their food is almost entirely aquatic–mainly fish, tadpoles and water beetles.

The Crested Basilisk *bottom left* lives among shrubs and trees near water, into which it drops as soon as danger threatens. It then either submerges or runs over the surface of the water. It can do this because of its light weight, the wide spread of its toes and the speed with which it runs. Because of this unusual ability, the Mexican name of this basilisk is 'river crosser.' Its food consists of plants and insects.

Second only to the elephant in weight– a large bull adult weighs about three tons–the Hippopotamus *left* inhabits the rivers of tropical Africa. Millions of years ago they lived in Europe.

One of the largest of all land mammals, the White Rhinoceros *right* of Central Africa and Zululand reaches a maximum height of about six and a half feet and a weight of approximately two and a half tons. A prehistoric rhinoceros, however, is estimated to have weighed some twenty tons! The 'white' in the Rhino's name does not refer to colour; it comes from the Afrikaans word for the wide, square mouth.

The Black Rhinoceros *below* of the Central and Southern African savannas is smaller than the white rhinoceros, standing about five and a half feet. Food consists of shoots and twigs of low bushes gathered by the rhino's prehensile upper lip. The Black Rhinoceros is the fastest of the pachyderms, reaching a speed of thirty five miles an hour in a charge.

Reaching a height of five feet and with a wingspread of some twelve feet the Maribou Stork, *top left* lives in Ethiopia and East Africa. It has a massive bill, pointed like a pickaxe, capable of inflicting a serious wound.

The eight feet tall Ostrich *above* of Africa is the largest living bird, weighing up to three hundred and fifty pounds. It can run at a speed of thirty miles an hour and in South Africa ostriches have been trained to race – complete with jockeys!

South America's equivalent of the African Ostrich is the Rhea *left*. During the breeding season it is aggressive and is shown here charging the photographer.

Two feet shorter than the Ostrich, the six foot Emu *right* of Australia is the world's second tallest bird. When the female has laid her eggs the male takes care of the incubation and rearing of the young.

One of the most brightly coloured of all Australian birds, the Gouldian Finch *left* is frequently kept by aviculturists.

A small area of Indonesia is the home of the Purple-naped Lory *right*. It is frequently kept as a pet by the local people.

The Sulphur-breasted Toucan *below* is an inhabitant of the dense tropical forests of Central America and has a penetrating croak which can be heard half a mile away. Despite its apparent solidity, the formidable-looking bill is porous and quite light.

One of the most beautiful birds in the world, the Green Peacock of South Asia *left* is often kept in captivity but it is a less hardy bird than the Common Peacock.

The Whooper Swan, *right* an inhabitant of Europe and Asia, measures some five feet from bill to tail and, at weights of up to thirty-five pounds, is among the heaviest of all flying birds. It can be dangerous and a blow from a wing can cause considerable damage.

Two-thirds of the height of the Rosy, or American, Flamingo *below* is taken up by its neck and legs. For it to retain the full brilliance of its colouring in captivity careful feeding is of the utmost importance.

The Senegal Parrot *left* of Central Africa inhabits the savanna woodlands and open forest. Their plumage blends well with the foliage. They are very noisy birds, frequently screeching and whistling and, when alarmed, these notes become harsh and raucous. The Senegal Parrot feeds on seeds, grain, fruits and leaf buds.

With its gaudy – but beautiful – plumage, the Blue and Yellow Macaw *right*, an inhabitant of South American forests, is a favourite in zoos. Its flight, with slow shallow wingbeats and long tail streaming behind, is surprisingly fast.

Hahn's Macaw *below* is the smallest of all the macaws and is widespread in the north-eastern part of South America. Several of them will sometimes huddle close together and indulge in mutual preening.

The Lammergeier *left* lives in Europe, Asia and Africa. It soars to immense heights and has been seen on Everest at a height of twenty-five thousand feet. The Lammergeier is also known as the 'bone breaker' from its habit of dropping bones on rocks so that it can extract the marrow with its hard, gouge-shaped tongue.

One of the largest of the carrion eaters is the Lappet-faced Vulture *below*. With its massive bill it can open carcasses that would prove too tough for other vultures. It is found throughout Africa but, not surprisingly, its main habitat is in the big-game areas.

Standing three feet high, the Shoe-bill Stork *right* of Africa has a wing spread of eight and a half feet and a huge clog-shaped bill with a hooked tip. The Arab name for this stork is 'Father of the Shoe'. The stork's favourite food is fish but small mammals, frogs, turtles, snakes and young crocodiles are also eaten.

Hundreds of the well-named Rainbow Lory *below* of Australasia sometimes fly together. There can surely be few more beautiful ornithological sights than such a 'flying rainbow.'

With age, the Twin-spot Wrasse, *top left* of Indo-Pacific waters, changes colour. Here it is shown when its colouring is at its best.

Tilapia *top right* are widely distributed in Africa south of the Sahara. In addition to being an important food in West Africa, they are favourite aquarium fishes and studies of their behaviour have shown several unusual habits. One of the most striking is that in some species the male incubates the eggs in its mouth, fasting until the young are ready to leave. It is believed that the fishes involved in the story of the miraculous draught of fishes were almost certainly tilapia. Canon Tristam wrote of seeing, in Israel, "Shoals of over an acre in extent, so closely packed that it seemed impossible for them to move, and with their dorsal fins above the water. They are taken both in boats and from the shore by nets run deftly round and enclosing what one may call a solid mass at one swoop, and very often the nets break." As in the Gospel story, a man is stationed at a high point on shore to spot the shoals.

One of the most colourful of the cichlids, a family of fishes which comprises some thousand species, is the Rainbow Cichlid *middle right* of West Africa. They live in rivers and lakes in Africa, the Americas and India. Cichlids are frequently found in aquariums throughout the world; most of them are easy to keep and they make attractive exhibits. Maurice and Robert Burton say: "The most spectacular aspect of cichlid behaviour is the way a male holding a territory will stop suddenly at its boundary as if bumping its nose against an invisible wall. Although it may swim towards it at speed, there will be the sudden stop at the boundary. Conversely, other fishes beyond the boundary recognise it in like manner and do not normally cross it."

The Veiltail *bottom left* is an ornamental variety of Goldfish. Raymond Chandler described such fish as having "telescopic eyes, froglike faces and unnecessary fins, waddling through the green water like fat men going to lunch."

The delicately coloured Queen Angelfish *bottom right* of the tropical West Atlantic looks conspicuous in an aquarium. It is, however, far less noticeable when drifting among corals and swaying sea vegetation.

Seahorses *left* are found in most of the world's seas but are most common in tropical waters. They are favourites in aquariums. The eggs are hatched in a brood-pouch on the belly of the male. Seahorses are the only fish with a prehensile tail, which they use to hold on to seaweed.

The Brown Discus or Pompadour Fish, *right* of Brazil, is very popular in aquariums. Soon after the young are hatched they cling to the sides of the parents, alternating between male and female.

This photograph *below* shows the 'human face' underside of the Thornback Ray of European coastal waters, which gets its name from the thorn-like projections embedded in the skin. The egg capsules are a common sight on sea shores and are known as mermaids' purses.

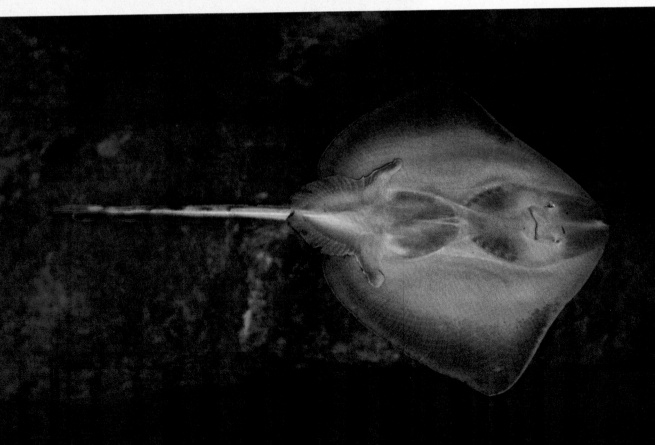

South America is the home of the Cotton-headed Tamarin *left*. It is a meat eater and its powerful canine teeth allow it to kill with ease such small creatures as mice and parakeets.

The Pygmy Chimpanzee, or Bonobo, *right* is a species distinct from its larger relative. It is found only in a small area of the Congo (Kinshasa) forests.

Gibbons *below* are the smallest of the anthropoid apes and they inhabit the rain forests of South-east Asia. Gibbons are characterised by their long arms which enable them to swing rapidly through the tree tops.

A baby Pygmy Chimpanzee, or Bonobo, *above* with Hanneke Louwman of the Wassenaar Zoo, Holland.

The Mandrill, *left* of the West African high forests, has the most strikingly coloured face of any mammal. It is the largest member of the monkey tribe and one of the longest lived; one that was kept at the London Zoo was believed to be 'about forty-six' when it died.

Tall trees in Madagascar are the home of the handsome Ruffed Lemur *top right*. Its long tail acts as a balancing pole during distant leaps from branch to branch.

Large troops of Gelada Baboons *right* live up to eight thousand feet on mountainsides in Ethiopia. The Gelada's striking appearance is sometimes enhanced by its habit of turning its upper lip inside out.

Gorillas, *left* of Central and West Africa, are the largest of the primates; some captive specimens have weighed over six hundred pounds and have had an arm-span of ten feet. The top weight achieved by Guy, London Zoo's famous inmate, was just under five hundred pounds–but he was then put on a diet! Gorillas are, of course, immensely strong; a single blow from an adult's paw can crack a man's skull. Despite their strength and frightening appearance–especially when angry–gorillas are peaceable animals and unprovoked attacks on humans are almost unknown.

The Orang-utan *below* (Malay for 'old man of the woods') is now confined to the islands of Borneo and Sumatra. The arms of an adult span nearly eight feet –a great help when swinging through the trees. Specimens have lived in captivity for over fifty years.

One of the best known and most popular of all zoo animals is the Chimpanzee *right* of Central and West Africa. Chimpanzees use simple tools, have great curiosity and appear thoroughly to enjoy learning tricks. Research has shown, however, that in learning ability orang-utans and gorillas are the equal of chimpanzees.

Nile Crocodiles *left and right* show their awesome jaws. They are among the largest of the crocodiles, reaching a record length of about twenty feet and weighing about one ton. By contrast, some of the smaller crocodiles measure only some four feet. Nile crocodiles are very dangerous, accounting for hundreds of deaths every year.

The American Alligator *below* is found only in the southern United States. It grows to nearly the same length as the Nile Crocodile. The American Alligator holds the record for longevity among crocodilians: at least fifty-seven years. One received in the Dresden Zoo, Germany, in 1880 was still alive in 1936 but its subsequent fate is not known. Although they are very similar it is possible to distinguish an alligator from a crocodile by the shape of the head; the alligator's is comparatively short and broad and the crocodile's is long and narrow–more so in some species than others.

Grévy's Zebra, *left* of East Africa, is the largest of the zebras and was named after the President of France–(1879-87)–who received the first specimens known to science.

The Greater Kudu *right* is found throughout most of the forests and bush-veld of Africa. The five-foot long spiralling horns are among the most handsome of any animal.

The Banded Duiker *below* lives in the mountain forests of West Africa, where its colouring helps to camouflage it by blending with the light and shade of the foliage.

The male Blackbuck *left* of the Indian plains is a handsome animal with two-foot long horns. The female is duller and is generally without horns.

Found only in small areas of the damp, mountainous bamboo forests of the western part of Central China, the Giant Panda *right* is rarely seen in zoos outside its homeland, but it is a very popular exhibit in any zoo fortunate enough to have one.

An inhabitant of the bleak windswept snowfields of northern North America, the Musk Ox *below* is well adapted for its rigorous environment. In addition to a long, dense fur coat, it has huge, widely splayed feet which act as snow-shoes. The 'musk' in the name derives from the smell of its fur.

Tallest of all living animals is the Giraffe *top left* of tropical Africa. It reaches a maximum height of about nineteen feet –which is four feet taller than a London double decker bus. A large bull giraffe weighs some one and a quarter tons. A kick from a giraffe can break a lion's ribs, but when giraffes fight each other they strike with their heads.

A charming sight at the London Zoo when Chi-Chi, the Giant Panda *right* became friendly with the occupant of the next compound, an Onager, or Asiatic Wild Ass. Sometimes the panda fed its friend by pushing food through the netting between them. Giant Pandas are the most valuable of all zoo animals.

The Roan Antelope *left* of Central and Southern Africa, is one of the largest of the antelopes; a big bull standing approximately five feet at the shoulder. These antelopes live in herds, sometimes fifty strong, each being lead by a master bull. A Roan Antelope was once timed by a car and was found to be reaching a speed of thirty five miles an hour. Smaller antelopes, however, can run much faster than this; the American Pronghorn Antelope can achieve sixty miles an hour for a short distance.

The Starred Tortoise of South Asia *left* is active in the early morning and late afternoon. Presumably such crepuscular activity is associated with the midday heat of its homeland, but the same midday pause is observed when the tortoise is in captivity in temperate climes.

The Loggerhead Turtle *right* is found in the tropical seas of both the Atlantic and Pacific Oceans. A large specimen sometimes weighs as much as eight hundred pounds. Both the turtle and its eggs are of commercial value.

Although named the Galapagos Giant Tortoise, *below* this particular creature is also found on other islands in the Indian Ocean. It is the largest living species of tortoise and weights of nearly five hundred pounds have been recorded. Tortoises are the longest-lived of all animals. A male Marion's tortoise which was brought, already adult, to Mauritius in the mid-18th century died one hundred and fifty two years later–but only through an accident!

South American Indians ferment the poisonous secretions from the skin of the Poison Arrow Frog *top left*. Arrows dipped in this venomous liquid are then used to kill small game.

Europe and Asia are the home of the Common Frog *middle left*. It is normally yellowish-green, but grey, brown, orange, and red specimens are sometimes seen. They are preyed upon by a multitude of animals–and are dissected by almost every biology student!

The South African Bullfrog *bottom left* is the largest in the country; some specimens reaching seventeen inches with limbs outspread, and achieving a weight of one pound. In addition to insects, they sometimes eat rats, crabs and small birds.

Living in the forests and swamps of Australasia, the Tree Frog *right* is also found in suburban gardens, where they catch insects. They are remarkably tame and can be picked up without, apparently, showing fright.

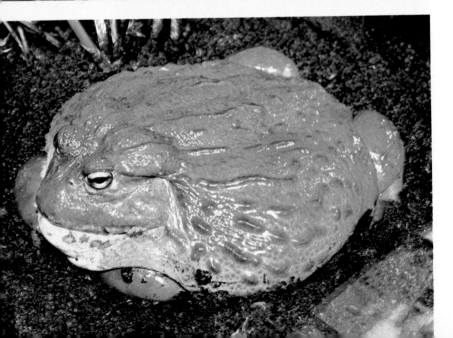

The Red Kangaroo, *right* of the open plains of Central, Southern and Eastern Australia, is the largest living marsupial. From tip of nose to tip of tail a big male measures about eight and a half feet and weighs nearly two hundred pounds. They leap for miles across the plains at speeds of up to forty miles an hour. In an emergency these kangaroos can jump forty feet and clear a fence ten feet high. Gerald Wood says: "In 1963 racing car drivers at a meeting at Caversham, Western Australia, were suddenly interrupted by a red kangaroo. Doing a steady thirty miles an hour, the marsupial bounded onto the track and leapt past cars as they dropped into low gear at a bend. Several alarmed drivers went into premature slides and others tried to frighten the animal away. The kangaroo took no notice and pressed on, beating all the cars round the bend and scattering spectators as it bounded back into the bush."

Probably the first marsupial to be seen by a European was the Dama Wallaby *left and below* of the coastal region of South Australia. The Dama wallaby is a shy animal and keeps well hidden during the day. If alarmed it thumps the ground vigorously with its hind feet together, like a rabbit. It is not possible to distinguish exactly between wallabies and kangaroos although wallabies are generally smaller.

57

The Cape Fur Seal *left* is found in the seas and on the islands off the southern coast of Africa. A large specimen measures nine feet and turns the scales at over six hundred pounds.

A Killer Whale *right* shows its armoury. These whales are found in all the world's oceans. They grow to thirty-three feet, weigh up to eleven tons, can swim at thirty-five miles an hour and dive to over three thousand feet.

There is only one species of Walrus *below* and its members live in the northern waters of both the Atlantic and the Pacific. A large bull grows up to sixteen feet and weighs one and a half tons.

Found as far north as South Georgia and Prince Edward Island, the Macaroni Penguin *far left, top* probably obtains its name from the long, straight yellow feathers which spring from its head.

The King Penguin *left* of Antarctica has a body temperature which befits its icy homeland; at 36.9°C., the lowest regular temperature of any bird.

Another member of the penguin family is the Rockhopper, *below left* which lives in both cold (Antarctica) and temperate (New Zealand) climates and is distinguished from other penguins by its red bill and yellow crest. It derives its name from the habit of hopping with the legs together.

Short-nosed Fruit Bats, *right* of which there are six species, are found in South Asia. Throughout the world there are about two hundred species of fruit-eating bats.

The Vampire Bat *below* of tropical South and Central America lives entirely on blood. Its teeth are specially adapted for piercing flesh, and coagulation of the blood flow is prevented by a chemical in the bat's saliva.

Vauka, the bull African Elephant *left* in the Opel Zoo, Germany, is one of the largest ever kept in captivity. Its height at the shoulder is about eleven feet. The African elephant is by far the largest living land animal. Record measurements are: twelve feet six inches high, thirty-three feet two inches long (tip of trunk to tip of tail) and over ten and a half tons in weight. All elephants have thick, sparsely haired skin *right* which is kept in good condition by bathing and wallowing.

The Indian Elephant *below*, which is found as far south as Sumatra, is distinguished from the African species by smaller ears, a domed forehead and a sloping back. It is also more easily trained to work for man.

INDEX

Alligator, American *(Alligator mississippiensis)*	45
Angelfish, Queen *(Holacanthus ciliatis)*	35
Antelope, Pronghorn *(Antilocapra americana)*	50
Antelope, Roan *(Hippotragus equinus)*	50
Baboon, Gelada *(Theropithecus gelada)*	41
Basilisk, Crested *(Basiliscus plumbifrons)*	20
Bat, Short-nosed Fruit *(Pteropinae)*	61
Bat, Vampire *(Desmodus rotundus)*	61
Bear, Brown *(Ursus arctos)*	18
Bear, Himalayan Black *(Selenarctos thibetanus)*	19
Bear, Polar *(Thalarctos maritimus)*	16
Blackbuck *(Antilope cervicapra)*	48
Boa, Green Tree *(Boa canina)*	15
Bullfrog, South African *(Pyxicephalus adspersus)*	54
Caracal *(Felis caracal)*	12
Cat, Leopard *(Felis bengalensis)*	12
Cat, Wild *(Felis silvestris)*	6
Cheetah *(Acinonyx jubatus)*	8
Chimpanzee *(Pan troglodytes)*	43
Chimpanzee, Pygmy *(Pan paniscus)*	39, 41
Cichlid, Rainbow *(Pelmatochromis)*	35
Crocodile, Nile *(Crocodylus niloticus)*	44, 45
Discus, Brown *(Symphysodon aequifasciata axelrodi)*	37
Duiker, Banded *(Cephalophus zebra)*	47
Elephant, African *(Loxodonta africana)*	62, 63
Elephant, Indian *(Elephas maximus)*	62
Emu *(Dromaius novaehollandiae)*	25
Finch, Gouldian *(Chloebia gouldiae)*	26
Flamingo, Rosy *(Phoenicopterus ruber)*	29
Frog, Common *(Rana temporaria)*	54
Frog, Poison Arrow *(Dendrobates auratus)*	54
Frog, Tree *(Litoria infrafrenata)*	55
Gecko, Madagascan *(Phelsuma madagascariensis)*	20
Gibbon *(Hylobates)*	38
Giraffe *(Giraffa camelopardalis)*	50
Gorilla *(Gorilla gorilla)*	42
Hippopotamus *(Hippopotamus amphibius)*	22
Iguana, Common *(Iguana iguana)*	21
Kangaroo, Red *(Macropus rufus)*	57
Komodo Dragon *(Varanus komodoensis)*	21
Kudu, Greater *(Tragelaphus strepsiceros)*	47
Lammergeier *(Gypaetus barbatus)*	32
Lemur, Ruffed *(Lemur variegatus)*	41
Leopard *(Panthera pardus)*	13
Leopard, Amur *(Panthera pardus orientalis)*	7
Leopard, Snow *(Panthera uncia)*	11
Lion, African *(Panthera leo)*	9
Lion, Asiatic *(Panthera leo persica)*	9
Lizard, Water *(Neusticurus)*	20
Lory, Purple-naped *(Lorius domicellus)*	27
Lory, Rainbow *(Trichoglossus haematodus)*	33
Lynx, Northern *(Felis lynx)*	6
Macaw, Blue and Yellow *(Ara ararauna)*	31
Macaw, Hahn's *(Ara nobilis)*	30
Macaw, Hyacinthine *(Anodorhynchus hyacinthinus)*	1
Mandrill *(Mandrillus sphinx)*	40
Musk Ox *(Ovibos moschatus)*	48
Onager *(Equus hemionus)*	51
Orang-utan *(Pongo pygmaeus)*	42
Ostrich *(Struthio camelus)*	24
Panda, Giant *(Ailuropoda melanoleuca)*	49, 51
Panther, Black *(Panthera pardus)*	12
Parrot, Senegal *(Poicephalus senegalus)*	30
Peacock, Green *(Pavo muticus)*	28
Penguin, King *(Aptenodytes patagonica)*	2, 60
Penguin, Macaroni *(Eudyptes chrysolophus)*	60
Penguin, Rockhopper *(Eudyptes crestatus)*	60
Ray, Thornback *(Raja clavata)*	36
Rhea *(Rhea americana)*	24
Rhinoceros, Black *(Diceros bicornis)*	23
Rhinoceros, White *(Diceros simus)*	23
Seahorse *(Hippocampus)*	36
Seal, Cape Fur *(Arctocephalus pusillus)*	58
Serval *(Felis serval)*	11
Snake, Grass *(Natrix natrix)*	15
Snake, Rat *(Elaphe)*	14
Stork, Maribou *(Leptoptilos crumeniferus)*	24
Stork, Shoe-billed *(Balaeniceps rex)*	33
Swan, Whooper *(Cygnus cygnus)*	29
Tamarin, Cotton-headed *(Leontocebus oedipus)*	38
Tiger, Indian *(Panthera tigris tigris)*	10
Tiger, Sumatran *(Panthera tigris sumatrae)*	4, 5
Tilapia *(Tilapia mariae)*	35
Tortoise, Galapagos *(Geochelone gigantea)*	53
Tortoise, Marion's *(Testudo sumeirii)*	53
Tortoise, Starred *(Testudo elegans)*	52
Toucan, Sulphur-breasted *(Ramphastos sulfuratus)*	26
Turtle, Loggerhead *(Caretta caretta)*	53
Veiltail *(Carassius auratus)*	34
Vulture, Lappet-faced *(Torgos tracheliotus)*	32
Wallaby, Dama *(Protemnodon eugenii)*	56, 57
Walrus *(Odobenus rosmarus)*	58
Whale, Killer *(Orcinus orca)*	59
Wrasse, Twin-spot *(Coris angulata)*	34
Zebra, Grévy's *(Equus grevyi)*	46

ACKNOWLEDGEMENTS

I am deeply indebted to the following zoos, aquariums and aviaries I have visited while taking the photographs for this book:

GREAT BRITAIN: Belle Vue, Manchester; Bentley Wildfowl Collection, Sussex; Birdland, Gloucestershire; Birdworld, Surrey; Blackpool; Bristol; Chessington, Surrey; Chester; Cleethorpes, Humberside; Colchester; Cotswold Wildlife Park, Oxford; Dudley; Flamingo Gardens, Bucks.; Howletts Zoo Park, Canterbury; Jersey; Kilverstone New World Wildlife Park, Norfolk; London, Regent's Park; Matlock Wildlife Park, Derbyshire; Paignton; Twycross, Warwicks.; Welsh Mountain Zoo, Colwyn Bay; Whipsnade. BELGIUM: Antwerp. DENMARK: Copenhagen. GERMANY: Bremerhaven; Cologne; Dusseldorf; East Berlin; Frankfurt; Hagenbeck, Hamburg; Hellabrunn, Munich; Opel, Frankfurt; West Berlin; Wilhelma, Stuttgart; Wuppertal. HOLLAND: Amsterdam; Rotterdam; Wassenaar. SWITZERLAND: Basle.

PHOTOGRAPHIC DETAILS

Some details of how the photographs were taken may be of interest. All were taken on 35mm. film, mainly Kodachrome. I use three Minolta cameras. I particularly like the XM Minolta, fitted with a plain screen which I find best for close-up photography. I have a selection of lenses; the Vivitar Series 1 70 -210mm. 3.5 with macro facility is excellent for zoo photography, where one subject may be 100 ft. from the camera, another a few inches. For fish and insect photography I use the Rokkor macro 50mm. 3.5.

Most of the photographs were taken by electronic flash. I prefer to use two flashes, one mounted on each side of the lens. Although I have used flash with automatic adjustment for distance I think a more accurate rendering of colour–particularly important in zoological photography–is obtained by using the more simple flash, where the exposure is a standard 1/1,000th sec. Why? Because with the automatic flash, exposures are often much less than 1/1,000th sec., sometimes as short as 1/50,000th sec., and such short exposures affect the colour rendering of the film. (Technically this is due to "reciprocity law failure"). And I find 1/1,000th sec. is fast enough for the vast majority of zoo subjects.

How do animals react to flash? Generally, they either ignore it or take only minimal notice. But not always. I have twice seen an oxpecker literally fall over when flash was fired at close range. I have also been told of an ostrich which dashed wildly about its enclosure after someone had fired a flash. But I believe these incidents to be exceptional. Need I add that no true animal-lover will put his photography before his subject's well-being. If he finds that flash is causing distress to any animal he should, of course, stop at once.

A few, a very few, zoos prohibit flash altogether, even in aquariums. But on request I have sometimes been allowed to use flash even in these zoos. At one aquarium, with such a rule, I was told that a fish had jumped out of its tank when a flash was fired. But providing I avoided this tank, permission to use flash was granted.